Reading between the lines

Piecing together the life of Elizabeth Boyd McDougall

by Shirley A. Serviss

Rowan Books

Rowan Books acknowledges the ongoing support of the Canada Council for the Arts, Edmonton Arts Council and the Alberta Foundation for the Arts.

The Canada Council for the Arts
Le Conseil des Arts du Canada

EDMONTON ARTS COUNCIL

The Alberta Foundation for the Arts

Alberta COMMUNITY DEVELOPMENT

COMMITTED TO THE DEVELOPMENT OF CULTURE AND THE ARTS

Editor for the press: Heather Marshall

Cover design: Jackie Boyko

Inside layout and design: Dianne J. Cooper in Georgia, Palatino, Verdana, Wingdings, Quark XPress 4.01, Mac OS 8.1

Printed and bound in Canada by Priority Printing, Edmonton, Alberta.

Published in Canada by Rowan Books, an imprint of:

ROWAN BOOKS
#410, 10113-104 St.
EDMONTON, AB T5J 1A1
Ph: (780) 421-1544 Fax: (780) 421-1588
email: jonrach@msn.com www.rowan-books.com

Canadian Cataloguing in Publication Data

Serviss, Shirley A.
Reading between the lines

Includes bibliographical references.
ISBN 0-9685257-3-3

1. McDougall, Elizabeth Boyd, 1853-1941--Poetry. 2. Missionaries' spouses--Alberta--Poetry. I. Title.
PS8587.E777R42 2000 C811'.54 C00-910678-2
PR9199.3.S455R42 2000

Dedicated

to my sisters

and all women

whose stories

remain untold

Foreword

My search for truth in the buried past can only be quarried by the act of imagination. On the basis of some information and a little guesswork you journey to a site to see what remains were left behind and to reconstruct the world that these remains imply. — Toni Morrison

I was once accused by my writing group of trying to rewrite the world from the stepmother's point of view, and I must confess this was my initial attraction to Elizabeth Boyd McDougall. Besides the fact that we were both stepmothers, I was drawn to Elizabeth by a number of other similarities. Her middle name, Ann (spelled without an "e") is also mine. She was born (at least by most accounts) in 1853 — 100 years before me. It was interesting to speculate what my life might have been like had I lived in another century.

Elizabeth Boyd McDougall is not to be confused with her mother-in-law Elizabeth Chantler McDougall who was married to the Methodist missionary George McDougall. The McDougalls came to what is now the Province of Alberta in 1862 and were apparently the first "white" family to take up permanent residence. "My" Elizabeth came west a decade later at the age of 19 as the newlywed second wife of their eldest son, John McDougall. John was 30 at this time and had three children from his first marriage to Abigail Steinhauer in 1864. Abigail was the daughter of Ojibwa missionary Henry Bird Steinhauer and Seeseeb Mamanawartum (Jessie Joyful), a Swampy Cree. Abigail's "sudden and unexpected death" at the Victoria Settlement (now Pakan, Alberta) was originally attributed to small pox, which had claimed the lives of several of his sisters the year before. Some have speculated it may have been a suicide.

Elizabeth was a distant relative John courted only briefly on a trip to Ontario following his ordination as a Methodist missionary shortly after Abigail's death. I can only imagine what it must have been like for the young greenhorn to try to fill Abigail's moccasins as wife, mother and missionary. For, like ministers' wives today, there would have been the expectation (and, in those times, the necessity) that the wife would play an active role in the work of her husband. Certainly the precedent had been set by John's mother who has been described as "the Madonna of the West."

Elizabeth Boyd's major claim to fame appears to be that she was "the first white woman in the Southwest." John and Elizabeth established the Morley mission in 1873 where they were joined by John's brother David, a trader, David's wife Annie and baby daughter.

Although a slim biography has been written about Elizabeth Chantler, I could find only passing references to Elizabeth Boyd's life among her husband's many published memoirs and the writing of other western Canadian historians. I'm not sure whether it says more about the man or the times that such a prolific writer could devote so little space to his two wives and his numerous children — three daughters with Abigail, one daughter and four sons with Elizabeth. The Glenbow Archives yielded numerous photographs of the McDougall family, speeches that Elizabeth gave in her later life and articles (often conflicting) that were written about her.

Aside from the "facts" I obtained from my research and have noted in this collection, I do not claim to have captured the Elizabeth Boyd McDougall some still living today knew and loved. My version of her life is informed by my own experience as a wife, stepmother, mother and westerner and my own experience of faith. I chose poetry as the most suitable genre in which to recreate her life because it allows me to fill in the gaps with my imagination and yet it still leaves gaps — between stanzas, between poems. My hope is that my "literary archaeology," as American novelist Toni Morrison calls her writing about slavery, brings to life a woman who deserves to be more than a footnote in history.

Contents

Looking for Elizabeth

Detective work

How do I trace a woman's life
whose footsteps have been
erased by snow, whose scent
has been effaced by time?

How do I read between the
lines of her husband's story,
decipher margin notes
written in invisible ink?

Must I take a magnifying glass
to footnotes to find her?
What if the lens
through which I see
makes her larger
than she was in life?

First clue

This index card in the archives
the closest I've found to her
fingerprints on history,
the first whisper I've heard
of her own words, the first
I've seen her mentioned
in her own right.

So few leads she has left me.
I don't even know if Eliza
was her preference or
Elizabeth shortened to fit
on this small card. Lizzie
I find her called in a book
on pioneer women. Wifey
in John's letters.

Did she believe his-story
was the only one worth telling?
Or did she simply clean up
after herself the way
good wives do
not knowing women like me
with time on our hands
would come after her
searching for crumbs?

Dinner in the W.W. Arcade

I track Eliza to the Hardware Grill
on Boyle Street, order braised bison
served with barley and wild rice.
I hunger for the taste of wild meat
between my teeth, but any residue of
game has been erased by "Asian glaze."

My entrée is as tender as domesticated
beef — neutered steers raised for
slaughter, fattened on ground grain.
Only the texture of binder twine
remains to suggest an untamed past.

Hammer handles on washroom doors
the only hint this restaurant with
its fine china and haughty maitre d'
was once a hardware store.

Divining

A diviner was used at Rundle's Mission to locate unmarked graves.

If I were a diviner,
I could walk this province,
wand of willow in my hand,
watch it wave like prairie grass
or wind in whispering aspen,
point me to artesian
currents of women's history
I know flow just beneath
the surface, find graves
of babies they birthed
alone and couldn't save,
divine the sacred places
where their secret hopes
and fears are buried,
witch wells they filled
with lonely tears.

Playing by ear

Mary Evans was the wife of James Evans, a Methodist missionary who served the north from 1840 to 1846.

Mary Evans brought her
piano all the way to Norway
House on Hudson Bay, by ship
from Montreal to England and
back again, too cumbersome
to take by canoe on rapid rivers,
too heavy to portage on the
backs of moccasined men.

Those lonely nights she
spent at the fort with James
again away, she could take
comfort in familiar chords,
the ivory keys as smooth as
china beneath her hands.

No lessons prepared these
missionary wives for the
lives they would lead,
the roles they would play,
in this discordant land.

Learning to read

Women's history is written in
freehand beading on buckskin
jackets, patterns of even stitches
through patches and carded wool,
loops of cotton crocheted into lace.
It follows rules of even rows
of vegetables in gardens, jars of
preserves on pantry shelves,
washing hung to dry in the sun.

Women's history is telegraphed
in the rhythmic scraping of hair
from a hide, the turning of a
butter churn, the scrubbing
against washboards or river
stones. It is a code we have
not learned to decipher or
trained our ears to hear.

Women's history is darned
into socks, punched into
bread dough like letters of
braille poked into thick paper
with a stylus. We are too blind
to read it. We miss the messages
written in recipe collections,
carved in the crusts of pies.

Women's history disappears
like meals placed before
hungry men, kisses on children's
cheeks, aging parents nursed
until they die.

Honeymoon Heading West

Kissing cousins

Elizabeth Boyd was a distant cousin of John McDougall's. He moved west with his parents in 1862 and married Abigail Steinhauer in 1864.

I was raised on tales of my cousin's
wild ways. His mother's rare and
much-anticipated letters the adventure
stories that sparked my dreams.

John has become one of them.
I hardly know my own son, with his
tanned skin, his long dark hair,
his beaded buckskins. He beats the
Indians at their own games, easily wins
races with his long, strong legs, his
team of wild dogs. He has outrun a
wounded bear, a charging buffalo.
I swear this boy of mine has nine lives
and thank the Lord that it is so.

I read the letters until I know them
off by heart, until this cousin
I barely remember becomes
as real to me as my own brothers.
When the message comes to say
he married an Indian girl,
I try to hide my dismay.
Whatever made me imagine
I would have a part to play in his
incredible adventures?

Family secrets

"Whilst my son was at the mountains, his wife died suddenly, and to us, very unexpectedly."
— George McDougall writes April 27, 1871.

A letter came to tell us of John's
"sudden and unexpected loss."
We just assumed the same pox
that claimed his sisters' lives
the year before had ridden
across the plains once more.

When he came east to find
another wife, I didn't think to ask
him for a cause of death, nor
did he choose to tell me one.
It wasn't rare for child-bearing
women to die young.

Eliza asks questions about the west

This is a found poem from Elizabeth's speech "Pioneering in Alberta" about a minister contemplating missionary work who questions John about the west. I've rearranged the questions, deleted some words and attributed the questions to Elizabeth.

I suppose there are rivers
to cross. *Some.*
How do you get over?
If you can swim, well
you will be all right. If
you can't, stick to your horse.

Is there a parsonage?
A log shanty with a mud
roof that sometimes leaks.
Can we keep a cow? *Once*
they come into the country.

Can we buy provisions out there?
Yes, good stuff.
How near is the store?
A hundred miles more or less.

Are there any doctors?
Some in Winnipeg.
How far away is that?
Eight or nine hundred miles.

How often will we get the mail?
Once a month if the weather is
good. You will get it when it comes.

Hope

I filled my hope chest with embroidered
pillowslips, crocheted tablecloths,
bone china teacups, tossed
apple peel over my shoulder to form
the letter J, slept with wedding cake
beneath my pillow and dreamed
a bearded man. My mother saw
him in my tea leaves, riding a horse.

I had not dreamed he would be
married before, have three
mixed-breed children for me to mother,
did not imagine myself living
in a shack with buffalo fat
in place of butter. I did not try
to cart the contents of my chest
out west. At times I fear
I've left all hope behind.

Virgin territory

For two weeks we travel
alone, sleep in a cradle
of boughs beneath a sky
gemmed with stars.
My new husband makes
his way through the wilderness
between my legs,
stakes his claim.
An experienced traveller,
he guides me to places
I've never explored,
translates my unspoken
fears with ease.

Baptism by fire

I drive the democrat while my husband
John rides on ahead, scouting the horizon

for what dangers he will not divulge.
He says I'll find out soon enough and soon

enough I smell the acrid smoke, see it
turn the sky to night. He lights a fire to

fight it back. We huddle in the creek,
barely daring to breath into our damp

handkerchiefs. The fire roars round
and we drive on over blackened ground.

It is the sting of smoke in my eyes
that makes me cry.

Friend or foe?

Our first sign of human life a band
of mounted Sioux, no trace of
welcome on their painted faces.

My husband waves me to stay back,
greets them with a gift
of bacon from his pack.

I'm glad my gleaming hair
is put up with pins, know it
would make too lovely a scalp.

How to make bannock without a baking board or rolling pin

Mix flour with salt and water,
baking powder if you have it.

Knead with hands until the size
of frying pan. Hand to husband
to hold by the fire until firm
enough to stand against a stick.
Turn to brown on all sides.

Serve with tea, bacon and butter
if you have any bacon or butter.
Otherwise eat with tea
meal after meal.

Make more each evening
when you set up camp in case
you don't see deer or ducks
to kill for meat.

Give thanks that you have
anything at all to eat.

Moving into new territory

Flora
Ruth
Augusta
Their words as awkward
on my tongue as the
wheels of the democrat
on this prairie trail.

Flora Ruth Augusta
Flora Ruth Augusta
Flora Ruth Augusta
I commit them to memory
as I trundle towards
motherhood a month after
meeting their father.
Try to imagine the tan skin
dark braids of my
ready-made daughters.

Flora Ruth Augusta
Their names become a refrain
I return to over and over
again as my mind wheels
round and round wondering
what welcome awaits me.

Sign language

"The entire prairie was like a book which men with sharp eyes could read."

— Iris Allan, The Boy In Buckskins

I am learning to read
the land like a book,
to decipher the tracks of bear
or buffalo, know how long ago
a herd passed this way,
the trails of large camps
moving together for safety's sake,
small parties intent on war.
To tell Blackfoot from Cree
by the prints of a travois
dragged behind a horse, the
sharp points of the two stakes,
writing parallel lines on the ground.

As foreign to me as Cree
syllabics, bent grass, broken
twigs, imprints in the dirt
become my new alphabet,
compose a language
I must learn to understand
this illiterate land.

River crossing

Winter comes too early with driving
winds that make me want to turn tail
rather than drive my poor horse
headlong into the slanting sleet.
Ice floats in the river we are to cross.
My husband lashes dead wood together
with shaganappi to make a raft,
impresses me with his craftiness.

Crossing a partly frozen creek, I lose
a wheel, break an axle. My husband
takes a willow sapling to make a pole,
splices it in place. We carry on.
Creak and groan, groan and creak,
the complaints of my three-wheeled
cart my only companionship.

I sing remembered hymns to keep
my spirits high. My breath forms
rings like smoke in the chilled air.
Who do I think there is to see
these signals of distress?

The dark side

This man I married
could have killed a man
that night he saw a human
shadow skulk between the
carts and herd of horses.
He shot to kill, looked down
the sights of his single-barrel
gun and willed him dead.

Clutching his shoulder,
the wounded man fled.
John grabbed a pole, gave chase.
I wonder what he would have done
if fear for his own skin hadn't
sent him running back to camp.
Beat him to death
like a dog without a soul?

At daybreak, he followed his
bloody trail to no avail.
Did he curse the man whose steps
he tracked, or plan to nurse him well?
He cannot tell me now. What
lawless land is this when even
Christian men play judge, condemn
a man to death for theft?

Distance

Even in sleep, my husband keeps
his own counsel. Speaks in Cree.
I wake to the guttural sounds of

a strange tongue, coming from
a husband I don't know well enough
to interpret. I am sandwiched

between buffalo hides and two
strangers. An Indian guide
sleeps silently on my other side.

Winter camping

Wind wakes us, rattles our tent, threatens
to blow it down — the wolf of winter at our door.
Cold permeates my pores. I try to hide
my trembling. By midnight, it's clear
we have to move before the blizzard
tears the tent apart.

The men remember a nearby grove
where we can shelter in the leeward side.
Numb from cold, we drag tent and poles
through drifts, build a fire, rebuild the tent.

John falls unconscious from the cold
at the first taste of tea, is gone for hours
his tongue as still as though he'd touched
it to steel. I keep the fire burning,
fear fuelling my vigil while the Indian sleeps.
I blanket my husband with my prayers.
He wakes at dawn. We strike camp
and carry on.

Dominion

Our horses hobble their way west,
legs bruised and bleeding from breaking
the hard crust of snow. They lift one
hoof at a time only at our cruel urging.

No vestige of trail shows the way. No
sign of oats or hay to cushion bones.
They grow thinner by the hour
if time exists in this vast dominion.

We impose our will, our dominion over
the beasts of the field. To stand still
would mean eternal rest beneath
a suffocating shroud of snow.

Last leg

Bundled like a papoose, pulled
in a cariole behind my horse,
I feel like a helpless child,
try to refrain from asking
Are we there yet? as I crane
to see what lies ahead.

My husband dances across
the snow on his sinew-
webbed feet, seemingly
undaunted by the plagues
this promised land
puts in our path.

I'm beginning to believe
he could part the Red Sea
with his calloused palms,
could conjure up
manna as plentiful
as flakes of snow.

Christmas dinner

Dinner this Christmas is
unlike any festive meal of
memory. Not the familiar
taste of my mother's basted
turkey, but unborn buffalo calf,
boiled and smoked. All eyes
upon me, I try not to choke.

After months of bannock,
rarely meat, my husband
eats with relish. Dismisses
my reticence to indulge.
You'll get used to this.
Tells me of other family
favourites: dried moose nose,
beaver tails.

His father reports that in
times of scarcity, Indian women
have eaten their own babies
to sustain themselves.
This piece of intelligence
hardly improves my appetite.

I savour every crumb
of real bread as though
partaking of the sacraments.

Second

Wife

Facing the past

It's only once I face her
grave that Abigail comes

to life as John's first wife.
I trace her death carved

into stone, feel burdened by
its possible prediction of my own.

Scarred for life

"The loss of a parent or husband must be deplored with blood. A finger is cut off, or the arm pierced with a sharp flint, and the deeper the incision the more sincere the sorrow."

— George McDougall's letter, Sept.2, 1862

My husband has a scar
carved over his heart
the shape of an A
too carefully drawn
to have come from the
point of an arrow.

A self-inflicted wound
made partly in anger,
partly to honour Abigail's
death in the tradition
of her people.

Red tears replaced
the ones he could not shed
so deep his guilt and sorrow
at such an ill-considered death.
The letting of his own blood
giving his terrible pain
an outlet, a tangible reason.

Aurora

Departed spirits dance across
the northern sky, so close we hear
the swish of their skirts
through the crisp air.

Forest and rock, ice and snow
glow with their heavenly aura.

Abigail, is that you up there
this clear night, haloed by light
like the angel you've become
in death?

Beaded buckskin

Dear Lord, forgive my jealous heart
each time I see the freehand flowers
she beaded on his buckskin jacket.
Each stitch pierces my own skin
far thinner than the hide of deer.

Dear Lord, forgive my evil thoughts
for wanting it to rot and fall away
for wanting him to shed his love for her
so I can cover him with mine.

Cross-writing

My mother's letters take as
long to reach me as
she carried me in her womb.
All the lessons she still has
to teach me condensed into
cross-hatched calligraphy
that fills the pages but not
the hollow her absence
leaves in my life as large
as the distance between us.

Morley Mission

Mirage

I rise early and climb to a hilltop
like Jesus going off alone to pray
weary of being on display.
All yesterday I tried to hide
my fear, surrounded by these
savages John is anxious to save
from their pagan ways.

From here I can see the blue
of the Bow River, the snow
of the mountain peaks,
breathe smokeless air.
Blessed by such beauty, I fall
on my knees in awe of this
rare glimpse of heaven.

Home at last

No ghosts haunt me in this two-room
house we built of whip-sawed logs
chinked with moss and roofed
with sod. Our floor – plain
Mother Earth – spares us the bother
of sweeping and keeping it clean.
Our few windows we cover in
deerskin pounded thin to let in light.
When we want to look out
we open the door. Our cupboard
is a packing case which serves
us well for we have little enough
to place on shelves: a frying pan,
a few tin plates. We sleep on a mattress
stuffed with dry grass beneath
Hudson Bay blankets and buffalo robes.
My first real home in the west.
A home my husband
has not shared with any other
wife. I'm as happy as I've
been in this new life.

Home alone

"My sister-in-law, Mrs. McDougall came out from Edmonton a few months later to live beside us... Our husbands would have to go for supplies some four hundred miles into the south to Fort Benton and we would be alone with the Indians for months at a time."
— Elizabeth's speech "Pioneering in Alberta in 1873"

The men have gone to Fort Benton
for supplies. How long till their return
we only guess. I wave until they're
out of sight and fight against my tears.
How I fear the months ahead
will turn to years.

Days pass slowly even though there's
lots to do. Nights drag out lonely
and long. I hold John's shirt
to my breast, breathe in the earthy
scent of his skin, try to hold on
to my hope he will come home.

Hospitality

"Two white men came and built a shack beside us...
They were well educated but not civilized."
—Elizabeth's speech "Pioneering in Alberta in 1873"

Two white men built a shack beside us.
It would be nice to think they could be
neighbours. They are educated men —
one English no less — but we have discovered
them to be more uncivilized than the Indians.
They keep their house so filthy, no Stoney
will darken their door, nor share any food
they prepare. No neighbours at all
would be better than having such men near,
our husbands far away. I'd say we have
more to fear from them than we do from
the Indians we've barricaded ourselves against
behind our stockade.

A true story

One evening as Annie and Eliza sat sewing by the fire, a dozen Blackfoot in war paint barged into the cabin. Annie told Elizabeth to walk out slowly, then run to the Stoney encampment and bring back a woman who knew several languages. Eliza came back with the woman and grabbed the axe. The interpreter convinced the Blackfoot to leave.
—CKUA School Broadcast

One day a Blackfoot warrior appeared at the door. Annie held him off with a gun and sang hymns to distract him, while Eliza went through the window for help. The brave grabbed a red dress from the baby's cradle and left.
—*Pioneer Women of Western Canada*

One day while David's wife was with her, two painted natives appeared at the door and wouldn't leave. While one of the ladies engaged the men in conversation, the other picked up John's musket and confronted them.
—Grant MacEwan's *And Mighty Women Too*

On another occasion, Mrs. John held off two armed Blackfoot braves with a shotgun while Mrs. David rode for help to the Stonies. An interpreter came back with the Stonies and persuaded the Blackfoot to leave.– Albertan 1/4/41

Suddenly one night after we had put the children to bed, the Blackfeet burst into our room. They were all painted and armed. We were dumb with fear. While I went for a woman who could talk some Blackfoot, Mrs. David got the shotgun and, in order to nerve herself and also to help me as I went forth into the dark to look for an interpreter, began to sing a

hymn *All Hail the Power of Jesus Name.*
I can hear her shrill tones yet, slow and loud, and with a shake in her voice as she sang.– Mrs. John McDougall, *"Old Times In Our Canadian Northwest,"* New Outlook, 9/4/27

As they sat sewing, the doorway darkened and Mrs. McDougall noticed three Indians outside. She said quickly to her companion, "Don't be frightened, but there are three Indians here with guns." The sister's baby lay in the cradle and as one of the Indians advanced toward it, Mrs. McDougall said, "He's going for the baby, but he'll not touch it. I'll knock him down first." It was not the baby he was after, but a little red dress lying on the foot of the cradle. He picked it up and examined it carefully, then laid it down. Mrs. McDougall remembered a double-barrelled gun which her husband had left. She had never shot off a gun in her life but she told her sister to get it. "Just to let them see we've got it," she explained. The Indians were very much interested in the gun and wanted to trade one of theirs for it, but Mrs. McDougall shook her head. She could not talk Blackfoot and the Indians could not talk English. So, thinking of an Indian woman near who could talk a little of both, she said she would go and get her. Her sister said she would do something to attract their attention so they would not see her go out. Just as Mrs. McDougall was wondering what her sister could do, she started to sing, and what do you think she sang? *Oh For a Thousand Tongues to Sing!*

— Nina M. Langford, "Women of Achievement" Onward Dec.1, 1928.

Last resort

Today two painted Blackfoot
barged into the cabin,
startled us at our sewing.
We gestured to the door,
but they camped on the floor
and showed no intention of leaving.

All the long afternoon, they
followed us with their eyes.
We tried to hide our fear,
pretend we expected our men
for supper, but night drew near
and still the warriors didn't budge.

"Annie get the gun." I finally
commanded in desperation.
I grabbed the axe as she took up
my husband's musket. Looking
as fierce as we could muster,
we marched them out the door.

What a savage I've become,
turning visitors out into the night.
Is my faith in the Lord's protection
so weak, I must take up arms
forsake the power of prayer?

Winter

nothing-but-snow

the Stoney word

for winter

so cold

words

turn to ice before

they are heard

if no one

is near

to hear

Chinook

"Chinook was an Indian beauty who wandered into the mountains in the dead of winter and became lost. Young braves hunted diligently for her but finally gave up and the young squaw was presumed to be dead. Then before the period of mourning had passed, a warm and kindly wind swept down from the peaks and took away the snow. This is the gentle breath of the lost Chinook."
Grant MacEwan, ***Between the Red and the Rockies***

We prayed for a break in the
bitter cold that whitewashed
the inside walls, drove the cattle
to shiver in the coulees, buried us
alive in the cabin.

The Lord answered our prayers –
miraculously melted
two feet of snow overnight,
turned winter to spring, caused
frozen birds to sing.

"Surely with such a sign as this
they will believe," I thought,
but I was wrong. They explained
away the warm winds as the gentle
breath of the lost Chinook.

I no longer mind if it is God or the
lost Chinook who melts the snow,
now I know I will be saved
from the demons who tempt me
to follow her footsteps.

Visitation

Many claim to see White Eagle
ride his stallion through the mist,
his white dog at his side. It's true
I thought I heard a horse give out
an eerie whinny, thought I caught
a glimpse of flowing robes
just round the side of Devil's Head.

It is the Devil's work to make me
think a dead man could ride
these hills again. Alone too many
months, it is my husband's horse
I strain to hear. Daily I bargain
with God for his safe return,
for respite from such
haunting solitude.

Change in seasons

John's love was like spring
arriving slowly almost without my
noticing, though long awaited.
Not with the suddenness of winter,
waking one morning to a white world,
but a slow thawing of grief,
green shoots of grass appearing
in the thatch of brown,
buds forming at the ends of branches,
bursting into sticky leaves.

When did I become aware of the
change in seasons? Was it when a
smile bloomed on his face as he
spied me standing at the door
on his return? When he turned back
and raised his hat in one last wave
as though a breeze lifted the leaves?
When he laughed at some remark
I made — joy gurgling in his throat
like a mountain stream?

Just as each spring seems
unlike any spring that ever came
before, the leaves so many shades
of green, the blossoms brighter
than they've ever been, he sees me
as though for the first time.

Topography

John knows this country
like his own body. Rivers race
through his veins. His heart
pounds like a herd of buffalo.
His ears hear the frequencies of
footsteps, the faintest stir of leaves.
His thighs are as solid as stone.

I run fingers over his skin to trace
the topography, map his body
on memory as though biting
designs on birch bark, try to
find my way in this foreign land.

Planting a garden

"Sow only with a waxing moon;
you're likely to have rain quite soon."
Sifting this dry soil between my
fingers a week before the full moon
I hope there is truth to my mother's tale.
I comb my long hair to line
the trenches as I have seen her do
to trap the bugs, enrich the earth.

"One for the rook, one for the crow,
one to die and one to grow." She cast
her seeds generously along her
long, straight rows. My few seed
potatoes, turnips and barley are too
rare to be reckless, I plant each one
with care. Cover them with prayer.

Picnic

A glorious day in a world of unexplored
beauty, we set duty aside, harness an ox,
and set off for a picnic. The children tumble
in the cart as we bump and squeak into the
valley to the bank of a small creek.

We are young and the slow step of the
old beast and the lumbering shake
of the old cart don't mar our fun in the least.

Heedless of the breeze, we light a fire
for tea, tie up the ox, turn back to find
the grass ablaze. We save the ox —
just slightly singed — and start for home,
urging a faster pace as flames race behind us.

All night the fire glitters like the
eyes of hungry wolves. We pray
the wind won't change and bring the blaze
towards our fort at the edge of the forest.

They say God looks after fools
and little children. It must be so
for just at dawn rain erases
the flames from the horizon,
the fear from our hearts.

Recipe for pemmican

Skin the buffalo brought in
by the men. Cut meat into
long strips. Hang to dry
by the fire. Turn as required.

Pound in a parchment hide
with a wooden flail. Sprinkle
with rendered grease. Mix meat
and fat. Don't cease until smooth.

Put into bags made from
buffalo hides, sewed with sinew.
May add dried berries if
summer has been bountiful.

Survival skills

My husband is grateful for the
meals of prairie chicken and
high-bush cranberries I prepare.
He even likes the tiger lily
bulbs I bake or boil or dry.

It is not hard to please a man
who lived for months on boiled bark
and moss made into stew
called rubaboo, who even
boiled his moccasins for soup
when times were lean.

Lost

"I little dreamed that I would never again in this world, look upon my living father." — John McDougall,
Opening the Great West

John cannot forgive himself
for not knowing his father
was in distress. All these years
they've communicated with a
single glance, read each other's
minds though miles apart.

Firstborn son, he was the one
who had his father's heart,
kept step to his father's drum.
They thought as one and now
John walks alone as lost
as he has ever been in all his
years in the wilderness.

Birth poem

Birthing
my first child
in this new land
demanded reserves
of strength I didn't know
were stored in my swollen
body. I wandered alone in the
wilderness, lost my way and moved
in ever smaller circles, returning over
and over again to a place of pain, until I
became a wild animal, down on all fours,
biting down on a sapling a Stoney woman
placed between my teeth. Push, Annie or
the mother of God told me, and I pushed
until I moved the whole mountain range
all the way to the sea. The ocean washed
down my legs as I birthed a white calf
I longed to clean with my tongue.
It is done. I have given John
a son.

Keeping vigil

There John's mother goes again,
walking to the top of the slopes
her long skirt sweeping
dust from the dying grass.

The days grow short again.
There's snow on the peaks,
and still no sign of George
her youngest son.

All last fall, she watched
and waited until an early
blizzard kept her housebound,
killed her hope they'd make it
home from Montana before the frost.

All spring she listened
for the bawl of cattle over
the call of killdeers, while she hung
the wash to bleach in the sun.

All summer she haunted the foothills,
keeping her silent vigil, scanning
the empty horizon for a boy
on horseback.

It could make you crazy,
this endless waiting, worse
than the fortnight we searched
for her husband's body,
already buried in snow.

Temptation

Too precious to eat, I cradle this rare
treat in my palm, turn the stem with my
fingers seven times for the seven years
I've yearned for a taste of home.

I touch its cool red skin to my lips,
inhale its unmistakable perfume,
so unlike parched saskatoons
that pose as fruit on the plains.
I'm in the orchard once again,
twisting apples from gnarled boughs
to store in barrels in the cellar.

I'm tempted to steal into the woods
with my treasure, reserve every
succulent morsel for myself, savour
every bite as reward for seven years
of bannock and pemmican, but
such selfishness is unbecoming
in a mother, a missionary's wife.

For one more day I will hoard my
prize, preserve it on a high shelf
to admire, before I slice it in slivers,
to share with my children a taste
of the Garden of Eden I left of my own
free will to dwell in the wilderness.

Missionary work

I have learned to pull teeth,
set broken bones, clean maggots
from wounds, speak by making signs.

I have learned to see men who have
murdered, stolen horses, had many
wives, as sons of God.

Faith

"Our trust was in God and in the Stoney Indians."
— Elizabeth McDougall

For forty days and forty nights
my husband scouted the wilderness
speaking to various tribes, preparing the way
for the coming of the Mounted Police.

Surprising us at home one early
autumn evening, he was there
when a dozen Blackfoot warriors
arrived at the door, in war paint,
armed with rifles and revolvers
expecting to find the womanfolk alone.

We prayed for deliverance and it wasn't long
before a small group of Stoneys came by.
Once again, under Providence, we escaped,
thanks to God and the Stoney Indians.

Modern miracles

I have stood on this hill
to see the stars and know that
somewhere not as far
my family lives (or dies)
while months go by without mail.

This morning we wait
with baited breath, listen for the
breeze to bring the wheezing
sound of steam that means
the train is on its way to Morley.

As miraculous as though
a tumbleweed caught fire
before my eyes, its black body
snakes around the curve,
crosses the river towards us.

“Praise God from whom
all blessings flow,” swells in
our throats, the notes
clear as killdeer song
in the spring air.

Tall tales

John tells tales taller than the
mountains: the miles he's walked,
the buffalo felled by a single shot.
Does he fancy himself another
David slaying Goliath with a
single smooth stone?

Does he think he must prove
himself worthy of me with the
foreskins of Philistines,
the souls of the heathen?
Is it God or his father
he's trying so hard to please?

Over all this land, men have
sung his praises. Doesn't he
understand there is no need
for him to beat his own drum?

King Solomon

*"Many controversies and disagreements,
petty and serious were brought to me for settlement."
— John McDougall,* ***Opening the Great West***

The preacher is expected to be
King Solomon. To decide which man
gets the woman or the horse.
To reinstate cast-off wives
in their husbands' favour.
Make peace between tribes.

How confident my husband grows
that he knows what is right.
At night he offers his verdicts
on my day-to-day concerns
without my asking. I wonder
how he thinks I manage all the
months he is away when I must
trust my own wisdom.

Praying John

Praying John they call him.
He finds the right words to say
the way a diviner finds a well.
Words spill from his tongue
like mountain water.

My prayer is silent. I hear
the wind pray without ceasing
through the willows, the chickadees
give thanks for spring, the buffalo
lament their ceaseless slaughter.

BUFFALO CHASE.

Reflections

Kindling

Holding a handful of grass,
John picks the shortest blade
to represent the whites.
It is weak and alone, like the
few missionaries or traders
now in the west.

He warns the bragging braves
around the campfire that if they
hurt the whites in any way
as they say they will, the fist
of grass in his other hand will come
with guns and ammunition.

I fear what he says is all too true.
Their days as masters of their land
grow few as herds of buffalo.
They are powerless to stop
the grassfire of settlement
that burns on the eastern horizon.
A fire I fear we have kindled.

Missionary position

John could see the wave of settlement
cresting on the horizon as clearly as
Noah knew the waters would rise
to float his ark. There was nothing
either man could do to stop the flood.

John could not bear to see the blood
of his Indian brethren fall like rain
for forty days and nights. Can he be
blamed for trying to reserve
them a place on the ark?

Eliza's view of Indians

This is a found poem. Elizabeth's comments have been taken from her speech "Pioneering in Alberta" and slightly rearranged. Only a few words have been added.

Perhaps you've heard it said
the only good Indian
is a dead one.
I myself don't like to hear
anyone speak this way.

It's true they aren't all saints,
but human beings like the rest
of us. There are good and bad
the same as any other race.

Some would say they were
very dirty people.
Perhaps this is true,
but let any one of us live
out on the prairie for months
without any soap. Would we
be any cleaner ourselves?

"However can you stand
living among those dirty Indians?
I could never have done it,"
said a guest the other day —
and her a minister's wife no less.
I said to her, "You are a good
woman and expect to go to heaven
when you die?" "I sure do,"
was her reply. "However are you
going to stay, for there are many
good Indians in Heaven?" was all I had to say.

Home fires

"When her husband travelled as a church superintendent, McDougall went with him by canoe and dogsled, despite having six children." — Canadian Encyclopedia entry under Elizabeth McDougall

Keep the home fires burning,
my mother-in-law advised
the role she played with George
away so often and so long —
not the way I want to live
with John.

There are fires burning
within me I want to stoke.
More Mary than Martha,
I want to follow the calling
of my own heart. To walk
in his moccasins, be at his
side not a shadow-
length behind.

Treaty Number Seven

You will not find my name
on the Treaty even though
some sources say I signed it.
I wasn't there that fateful day
to share tea in a tent
with the colonel's wife,
to witness the event.

I am a witness to the way
their trust in us has been betrayed.
Thou shalt not roam the land
without a pass, hold a sundance
or a sweat. Thou shalt not even
sell a cow without permission.
Who wrote these rules in stone?

Claim to fame

They call me the first white woman
in the southwest. What a strange

claim to fame, as though the colour
of my skin means I'm not kin

to the Stoney women, bought with
blankets or a herd of stolen horses,

bartered by men consumed by
whiskey to pay gambling debts.

As though blood every bit as red
doesn't flow between my legs

with the phases of the moon,
as though I'm somehow set apart,

not part of the land I've learned
to call my home.

Canoe diary

This is a found poem, taken from a diary Eliza kept on a trip northeast of Lake Winnipeg in 1902 with John, her four-year-old son Douglas and two young Native men John and Willie. Words have been deleted and sometimes rearranged, but no words have been added. Writing this poem on Monday, July 21, 1997, I realized the days of the week matched the dates for 1997 and decided to run my own diary parallel to Eliza's to reflect on her life and contrast it with my own.

1902 ***Monday, July 21*** **1997**

We feel lonely at parting
with our friends. A guide
will take us as far as he
knows and then go back.

Missing my daughter away
at church camp for the
first time. Hope her experience
in Guides will spare her
homesickness.

Tuesday, July 22

This morning made our
first muskeg portage.
This afternoon heavy hail.
Made 13 portages all told.
This ended a hard and
tiresome day.

Wednesday, July 23

Crossed a long lake. Had a
lovely sail with fair wind
which gave our men a rest
from paddling. This is as far
as our guide comes with us,
as far as he knows the way.
Now we start into a vast
country, find our way the
best we can.

Corduroy clouds today.
Saw them first reflected in the
creek far below the bench where
I drank coffee in the sun. A
thunder storm by supper.
Turned off my computer for fear
the power goes out.

1902 **1997**

This is a dreadful country
to travel in without a guide.

Thursday, July 24

We have come a long way
across a very long lake called
Deer Lake. Made four portages.
Now camped for the night
beside a high waterfall —
beautiful to look at. All very
tired and ready for rest.

*Walked to the highway
and back to stretch
my legs. The canola fields
glow in the setting sun.
The sky a lovely pink.
Think I heard coyotes
yelping by the creek.*

Friday, July 25

Portaged past three long rapids
and wildest falls and ran two
rapids. This is a wild country—
nothing but forest, rock and
water. We came far this
afternoon; had a thunderstorm.
Very late when we camp
for the night.

*Birthed my daughter ten years
ago today. Brought her home
the day before the tornado.
Could have called her: Wind-
Blew-In, Green Sky or Long-
Awaited.*

Saturday, July 26

Made three rough portages
through thick brush, over logs
and very wet. Travelled all day
in the wrong direction. Pitch
camp in a very quiet lonely
spot for Sunday. I am glad
to rest a little. Have done my

*My skin turns darker by
degrees each day of sun, just
as the saskatoons become a
deeper shade of purple. They
are almost ready to be picked
for pie and I am eager for this
taste of summer.*

1902	1997

washing for this week. We must
be clean even in the wilderness.
This is my first bad headache
on the trip. I hope I feel better
soon for there is no time to
be sick on an outing like this.
To make things worse the
sandflies are awful. It is a
great blessing that a little smoke
will drive them away.
If it wasn't for that
one would go crazy. We will
be smoke dried and as brown
as gypsies, all this by the time
we get out of this country—
if we ever do.

Sunday, July 27

We are having a quiet time
alone here with ourselves. This
is anything but a pleasure trip
for it is up at four and five
o'clock and we pitch camp late.
We have spent another long,
lonely day but enjoyed the rest
and hope to be better for
it all the week.

It is four o'clock and still we have
not found the way. We are trying
another course.

Walked down to the river.
Nearly eaten by mosquitoes.
Found wild strawberries
hidden in the grass to
sweeten the walk.
There are enormous
mushrooms everywhere
after rain. Wish I knew if
they are safe to eat.

1902 **1997**

It is not pleasant to feel
uncertain of our way but we
have faith something will
turn up soon to guide us
out of this lonely country.

Tuesday, July 29

Heavy rain last night.
Everything wet. We are
fighting the sandflies.
They are trying on one's
patience. Another portage
three miles long, five miles
of it today. Douglas is a
good walker. Once in a
while he will say, "Pa! Give
me a boost; I am tired."
Our bill of fare today was tea
and bannock, first meal;
second meal: bacon,
bannock and tea; third meal:
bannock, butter and tea; fourth
meal: tea and bannock. We
always have four meals a day.

The warmest day of
summer and I'm
spending it inside the
smoky dark of a casino.

I can't help but think how
horrified you would be
with me, Eliza,
condoning this vice,
spending this nice day
watching people play
black jack, lose more
than they take away.

Wednesday, July 30

Off again in our canoe,
cross a lake. Another portage
but not a long one. Soon
back in the canoe.
On another lake we find to

Picked Saskatoons today
to make a pie. Bending the
high branches down to milk
the berries into the tin pail
I'd tied to my waist to free

1902

our astonishment that we
are just where we were on
Monday. We have taken a
circle around and come
back to the same place.
We feel rather serious.
This is a dreadful country
to be lost in. Our friends
would never know what had
happened to us. But we still
have faith in God.

1997

my hands, it was as though
I could reach through
time and join Eliza
in the berry patch.
Women's work spanning the
century that separates us.
The meditative nature
of berry picking connecting
me to God.

Thursday, July 31

Trying to find another way
out, trying a new trail.
Cross a lake and paddle
down a long river. Made
three portages and camped for
the night. All tired out
and glad to rest.

Friday, August 1

Are following Indian trails
everywhere. All these days
we have not seen an Indian.
I am cooking a chicken the first
we have seen. With so many
rivers and lakes around we
expect ducks but they
are like the Indians
out here—
few and far between.

1902 **1997**

Saturday, August 2

Failed to find the way. Start in a new direction but heavy wind and rain become so wild, force us back to shore. Has been showering all day. Make up our minds to rest today and over Sunday. I have done my washing and made bannocks. The men are busy cooking and mending their boots. My husband has been writing in his book. Douglas is having a fine time playing on the beach when it is not raining.

We feel lonely and anxious in this vast wilderness, not knowing where to go. Of course we could go back by the way we came, but that is not what we are here for. If only we could find an Indian to help us out, how thankful we would be.

Went to Heritage Day today. Parked by the Zoo and walked across the new bridge. I bought bannock at the Native pavilion to share in the shade. My daughter got her hair braided, wrapped with beads and embroidery thread.

Sunday, August 3

A very long, lonely day. A lost dog came to our camp. We were very glad to see him.

1902 **1997**

He made us feel as if
there was someone else in
this country besides our
party. The dog is settled
down beside us. He seems
glad to have company too.
I am glad Douglas and I
are here with my husband.
What a lonely time he would
have had!

He says I will have a good rest
from cooking and housework
in our home. But I think we
would all enjoy having tea in
our own home this evening,
even if I cooked it myself.

Monday, August 4

We start out feeling better for
our rest hoping to find the
portage we have been
looking for, for the last ten
days. After travelling four
hours we came to a long
portage. How thankful we
all feel. We think we are
now on the right way. We make
half the portage and camp.
It takes the men all
afternoon to get the loads

1902

this far. They tramped a
good thirty miles each and
had a very hard and tiring
time through muskeg.
Your feet go away down into
the cold water. We had to sleep
in our canoe tonight the muskeg
was so bad, so wet. There are
mosquitoes and flies
by the hundreds.

1997

Tuesday, August 5

Oh what a walk in the chill,
grey morning! Through muskeg
and water. It makes Douglas
and me very tired, but we keep
going until we reach the end
of the twelve mile portage.
Four hours and thirty seven
minutes steady tramping.
In our canoe again on a large
lake, we go a little way
and my husband says, "I think
that is a house over there."
We paddled in. "What lake
is this?" my husband asked.
"Sandy Lake." The big lake
we thought we had left far
back beyond the portage.

*Another sunny summer day. I
take my coffee to the lawn
swing, rock back and forth
improving my tan,
return to where I began
without making any
progress.*

1902 **1997**

But never mind. We have
found a guide to take us
through to Island Lake over
endless rivers and lakes a hun-
dred miles straight north.

We can rest and not strain
our eyes for fear we might
miss something that would
help us out of this country.
We will rest tonight, thanking
the Lord for his care
the past weeks.

Backward Glances

Muscular Christianity

"Nevertheless during its crucial era what has been called McDougall's muscular Christianity, coupled with his vigour as a frontiersman, served the West well."
— James G. MacGregor, ***A History of Alberta***

You were a wandering man, John, as nomadic
as the Indians you tried to convert. There's a
story told of how you bragged of riding fifty miles
a day, day in and day out, week in and week out
and someone asking, "Where the hell was you gain'?"
I'm tempted to ask the same thing.

Were you driven by your father's decree you must
go on until the last wigwam was entered, the last pagan
brought to the feet of Christ? Or was it their very
company you craved? You didn't write as much
about the heathens you'd saved as your joy when they
accepted you as one of them.

Was it the calling of the Lord that lured you
to the wilds, or the calling of the loons, whose tunes
you loved as much as hymns? Was it souls you were
after, or buffalo tongues as you raced across the open
spaces, buckshot stowed in your cheeks? You took
as much pleasure in baptizing the unconverted—
the greenhorns you guided across rivers, hanging
to horse tails, swimming for their lives.

True, you ended each day with prayers,
faithfully honoured the Sabbath on your journeys,
but as you observed "anyone who drove as hard
for six days, was glad enough to rest on the next."

Role models

"From this point forward the husband and wife story became so interwoven that it was difficult to relate about one without talking about the other." — Grant MacEwan ***...and Mighty Women Too***

I was not Eve, tempting Adam
to taste the Tree of Knowledge.
John was the one who opened
my eyes to the vast prairie skies.

I've been compared to "Sarah of old,"
following Abraham in search
of a new land, but John had been here
before; he knew the way.
Nor was I barren; it wasn't long
before my young body gave him
another daughter and five sons.

I was not Lot's wife, looking over
my shoulder at all I'd left behind.
Though often lonely, I had little
longing for the past.

I longed to be Priscilla, sharing ministry
with Aquila which is why
I left my fireside to canoe
over rapids through uncharted
land, swatting at sandflies.

Sources

Allan, Iris. ***The Boy in Buckskins***. Saskatoon: Western Producer Prairie Books, 1978. This book, first published in Edmonton by the Institute of Applied Art Ltd. in 1959, tells of the early life of John McDougall. It is a dramatized account based on Allan's reading of many of the books included in this bibliography. It was in Allan's book that I read of John being asked to preach a Christmas sermon to the officers and men of the Hudson's Bay Company and finding himself unable to address them in English, so long had he spoken Cree. It led to my speculation expressed in the poem "Distance" that he might dream and sleep talk in Cree. Her description of Peter Erasmus teaching John to read the land led me to imagine John passing this knowledge on to Elizabeth in my poem "Sign language." Allan also describes the beaded jacket Abigail made so lovingly for John that is featured in my poem "Beaded buckskin."

Bohnec, Ruth. ***Pages from the Past***. Edmonton: Alberta Education, 1979. This author claims Elizabeth helped the Native peoples and was active in setting up schools and a hospital, concluding that she worked very hard for the church. I wasn't able to verify her involvement with the schools and hospital elsewhere, although it stands to reason that she would have been. A recipe for fire water is also included in this publication: a quart of whiskey, a pound of tobacco, a handful of red pepper, a bottle of Jamaican ginger and a quart of molasses. This was mixed with water and then heated to the boiling point.

Caroll, Joy. ***Frontier Days***. Toronto: Natural Science of Canada Ltd., 1979. This book is part of a series entitled *Canada's Illustrated Heritage*. covered the pioneer days from 1840-1860 prior to Elizabeth's time in the west, however I was interested in Paul Kane's observations from his travels and incorporated some of those details into the description of their meal on Elizabeth's arrival.

Fowke, Edith. ***Folklore of Canada.*** Toronto: McClelland & Stewart, 1976. According to Fowke, the McDougalls were gifted storytellers and she excuses their tendency to exaggerate as "romancing, a form of humour" rather than lies because "a lie is a falsehood to deceive people."(176) "They were good men—never drank, never smoked, never swore. They just romanced." (175) A number of Dave McDougall's stories are included.

Grant, John Webster. ***Moon of Wintertime***. Toronto: University of Toronto Press, 1984. This book paints a less than flattering picture of John McDougall. He includes John's justification for the wanton slaying of buffalo as necessary to settlement as it left acculturation as the only prospect of survival for the Natives. Christianization was seen as an indispensable component. On a lighter note, he describes John startling his fellow ministers at a session of the Methodist general conference when he chose to sleep in a tent outside the city rather than accept a billet.

Hardy, W. G. (editor-in-chief). ***Alberta Golden Jubilee Anthology***. Toronto: McClelland & Stewart Limited, 1955. This book provided more information on the first Elizabeth (George McDougall's wife) than the second. It told how she held services for the women, nursed the sick and acted as a mediator in disputes and in later life continued to visit the sick and lonely and mother all—especially the children of the orphanage.

Hungry Wolf, Adolf & Beverly. ***Indian Tribes of the Northern Rockies***. Skookumchuck: Good Medicine Books, 1989. This book was useful particularly for the photographs and stories. It also contained a report on the meeting prior to the signing of Treaty Number Seven and a copy of the treaty and the names of the signitaries—although not the names of the witnesses. "When Treaty Seven was signed in 1877, the Stoneys placed their future in the hands of the McDougalls, who were their trusted advisors and interpreters. They thought these spiritual leaders were working for the Creator and for the Stoney people, without realizing or understanding the wider view of the McDougalls' long-range interests, to see Western Canada settled, civilized and Christian." (53)

Hutchinson, Gerald and Stephen Wilk (editors). ***McDougall Reflections: The Future of The Indians of Canada by The Rev. John Chantler and Elizabeth Boyd McDougall.*** Calgary: McDougall Stoney Mission Society, 1996. This was the first published writing I had seen of Elizabeth's although I later discovered several published articles in the Glenbow files. It was exciting to see her perspective included, although, interestingly it was entitled (presumably by her) in a self-deprecating way "Just a few Sentences About the Indian..." A profile of the Rev. Dr. John McDougall is included in the booklet, but no profile of Elizabeth. Their recognition of the way in which settlement exploited the wealthy domain of the Natives is valuable reading in contemporary times.

Jenness, Diamond. ***Indians of Canada***. Toronto: University of Toronto Press, 1977. This book included information on the religion, folk-lore and traditions, interaction of Natives and Europeans as well as on specific tribes of the Plains. I read it in my continuing attempt to understand what appeal Christianity would have to a people steeped in their own spiritual beliefs and rituals.

Kroetsch, Robert. ***Alberta***. Toronto: Macmillan Company of Canada, 1968. This was perhaps my first encounter with any negative reflections towards the McDougalls. Kroetsch blames both Father Lacombe and the McDougalls for selling out the Indians. I was surprised that in most of the history books I found about Alberta, the McDougalls received little or no mention at all, and certainly no credit (either positive or negative) for their contribution.

MacEwan, Grant. ***...and Mighty Women Too***. Saskatoon: Western Producer Prairie Books, 1975. Although his title makes women seem like an afterthought (which it was, coming as a "companion volume to *Fifty Mighty Men*") MacEwan sings the praises of many women who contributed to the quality of life in Western Canada—Elizabeth Boyd McDougall among them. MacEwan's biography of her was my first introduction to this woman who has so captured my imagination; I am grateful to him for rescuing her from oblivion. His description of their trip west inspired many of my poems.

MacEwan, Grant. ***Between the Red and the Rockies***. Toronto: University of Toronto Press, 1952. It was here that I encountered the legend of the lost Chinook which I incorporated into the poem I was writing about chinooks as a way to suggest how lonely Elizabeth must have been.

MacDonald, Robert. ***Mission to the Stoneys.*** Calgary: McDougall Stoney Mission Society, 1997. This booklet basically recounts in brief the contribution made by a number of Methodist missionaries—the McDougalls included. It inspired one of the poems—a comparison between Elizabeth and other women in the Bible. "Like Sarah of old, Elizabeth Boyd McDougall followed her husband's call, and like Sarah travelled into an unknown land relying on her husband's knowledge and God's guidance." (24)

Maclean, John. ***McDougall of Alberta***. Toronto: The Ryerson Press, 1927. Elizabeth gets little mention in this tome subtitled *A Life of Rev. John McDougall, D.D. Pathfinder of Empire and Prophet of the Plains*. Abigail, his first wife, receives even less notice and is not once referred to by name.

McDougall, John. ***In the Days of the Red River Rebellion***. Edmonton: University of Alberta Press, 1983. This reprint of a book originally published in 1903 in Toronto by William Briggs, ends with an account of his honeymoon trip with Elizabeth. It presents a portrait of a more vulnerable man than some of his other writings, speaking of his intense dislike of being alone, his shame at his display of weakness when he lost consciousness in front of his new wife, and a very touching description of his brother David as a first-time father. "A fonder or more attentive one I had never seen. The little tot had but to move or whimper and David was all alive, be it day or night...I was proud to witness such affection and true manhood in my brother." (298)

McDougall, John. ***Opening the Great West***. Calgary: Glenbow-Alberta Institute, 1970. The introduction by Ernest Nix which speculates on John McDougall's motivations for going into the ministry (to please his father) and his tendency to brag (to cover up his own inferiority for a lack of formal education) were perhaps the most interesting. John McDougall rarely refers to Elizabeth, and then only as "my wife" or "Mrs. McDougall." His concluding comment is telling: "Truly she, as the wife of the wandering pioneer missionary, had passed through many strange and startling experiences during the eventful years which had intervened." (61)

McDougall, John, edited by Thomas Bredin. ***Parsons on the Plains***. Don Mills: Longman Canada Limited, 1971. This is an edited version of John McDougall's three books: *Forest, Lake and Prairie*; *Saddle, Sled and Snowshoe;* and *Pathfinding on Plain and Prairie.* I found this to be a captivating book and was quite amazed by the incredible physical feats John performed in order to survive in the west. (I read this book prior to reading any references to his tendency to make himself larger than life or I might have been less impressed.) His desire to please his father also came through very clearly; every word of praise he ever received (it would seem) is recorded. My poem "The dark side" was inspired by one of his stories from this book. John's use of a handful of grass to make his point about the need for peace treaties that appears in my poem "Kindling" also came from here.

McDougall, John. ***Pathfinding on Plain & Prairie.*** Toronto: Coles Publishing Company, 1971, was originally published in Toronto by William Briggs in 1898. This book begins with John's marriage to Abigail and contains the only reference I have read in his writing that concerns her nationality: "I was particularly pleased to note the manner of both my sister and brother towards my wife. The fact of her being a Native did not in anywise affect the kindliness of their conduct towards her, for which I was very thankful." (98) In typical fashion, John gives only a paragraph to the birth of his first daughter—less mention than his purchase of chickens at the Roman Catholic Mission or his many other adventures. This book displays a more judgmental stance towards paganism and more evangelical fervor than is in evidence in John's other writings.

MacGregor, J. G. ***Blankets and Beads***. Edmonton: Institute of Applied Art, 1949. My poem "Tall tales" was inspired by MacGregor's comment: "These were the days of great open spaces, long distances, big men and tall tales. It is to be surmised that one, at least, of the missionaries indulged in tall tales of a Munchausen variety now and then. He performed prodigious feats of travel by dog team and on horseback, and killed buffalo with an infallible precision." (219) I was not sure how to read one of his other statements: "It was the good sense of the missionary that persuaded the Natives to face the inevitable, and to allow himself to be reduced from Lord of the Plains to an agricultural drudge on a reserve, instead of being ruthlessly wiped out, as he would have been, had he chosen any other course." (220) Was he being ironic? Damning with faint praise?

MacGregor, James G. ***A History of Alberta***. Edmonton: Hurtig Publishers, 1972. MacGregor is not particularly complimentary to the McDougalls in this book either, but does concede that "Nevertheless, during its crucial era what has been called McDougall's muscular Christianity, coupled with his vigour as a frontiersman, served the West well." (86). He also includes quite a detailed description of John and Elizabeth's trip south to Morley—named after Rev. Dr. Morley Punshon, a well-known Methodist minister from whom McDougall had secured endorsement to establish the mission. It is interesting to note that Morley was known by the Natives as Mun-u-chaben—the place from which wood is taken. (Alberta History, Summer, 1992)

Newton, Elsie. ***Elizabeth McDougall***. Aldergrove: Frontier Publishing Ltd., 1978. Subtitled "Madonna of the Plains," this chapbook clarified for me my confusion between the two Elizabeths. The first—Elizabeth Chantler McDougall—made a considerable contribution through her teaching, nursing and preaching in the absence of her husband. A refrain from this book fueled my poem "Home fires." Newton's description of the senior Elizabeth waiting for her son George to return from Montana inspired my poem "Keeping vigil." George Jr.never did make it home; he died of pneumonia and was buried in Montana.

Ross, Rupert. ***Dancing with a Ghost***. Markham: Reed Books, 1992. Ross's exploration of Native reality helped me to better understand the reception the missionaries received (not to mention how the actions or the presumed inaction of the natives continues to be misinterpreted based on our own values and ethics). The chapter on Native spiritual beliefs was particularly helpful.

Simon, Steve. ***Healing Waters***. Edmonton: University of Alberta Press, 1995. Simon's collection of photographs and commentary on the annual pilgrimage to Lac Ste. Anne gave me a better understanding of the relationship between Catholicism and Native spirituality, and made me even more bewildered about the appeal of the Methodist version of Christianity.

Smith, Barbara. ***Ghost Stories of Alberta***. Toronto: Hounstow Press, 1993. Smith tells the story of Chief White Eagle of the Stoney tribe, who led his people to safety in the Morley area, defeated by the Cree and Blackfoot. Mortally injured in another attack, he ordered his warriors to bury him at the peak of a nearby mountain. As they prepared his grave, they caused an avalanche which killed the attacking tribe. According to legend, the Chief still rides through the mists, leading me to speculate in my poem "Visitation" that Elizabeth might have seen him as she scanned the horizon for some sign of her husband's return from one of his many trips.

Swenson, Sally. ***Who Is Abigail?*** Ottawa: Self-published, 1996. Swenson's search to discover more about the life of her great-grandmother, Abigail Steinhauer McDougall, particularly her questions about the circumstances surrounding Abigail's death, changed my perspective on Abigail and consequently Elizabeth's reflections on her predecessor began to take on a different tone. To some degree, Swenson's writing also allowed me to be more critical of John, particularly of his long absences from home.

Van Kirk, Sylvia. ***Many Tender Ties***. Winnipeg: Watson & Dwyer Publishing Limited, 1980. I read this book on women in fur-trade society many years ago. It was interesting to go back and re-read references to the missionaries more closely. It also provided a rather disenchanting view of the way the Methodist religion was meted out to the Native people.

Other sources/resources

Father Lacombe Mission in St. Albert. Touring this mission gave me a greater sense of walking in John McDougall's footsteps since I knew he had once been there. The interpreters also provided useful information on methods of tanning and beading and I was able to see deerskin parchment which was used to cover windows in the McDougall home (glass having to be shipped from England in barrels of molasses).

Glenbow Archives in Calgary. There is a file of newspaper clippings about Elizabeth, many written at the time of her death as well as copies of several of her published articles. I also found the diary she kept on a trip northeast of Lake Winnipeg in 1902 with John, her four-year-old son Douglas and two young Native men, John and Willie. I deleted some words and rearranged others to turn it into the found poem "Canoe diary." It should be noted that the newspaper articles are full of inaccuracies and omissions, so the information contained in them should not be relied upon. The archives also has photo files with many pictures of the McDougall family. Among the McDougall records, there is a file of speeches and notes for speeches that Elizabeth gave. Care should be taken as it also contains speeches given by her sister-in-law Annie McDougall (David's wife) and the two should not be confused.

Rundle Mission. Touring the Rundle Mission with Gerald Hutchinson inspired many of my images. His description of the use of a diviner to locate unmarked graves led to my poem "Divining." He also introduced me to the speculation that Abigail's death was a suicide.

McDougall, George. Unpublished letters. George's letters provided useful details about day-to-day living, the landscape and his attitudes towards the Native peoples. (He seemed to view their spiritual beliefs with much less enthusiasm than did his son John.) His letter dated Sept. 2, 1862, provided the inspiration for the poem "Scarred for life." In it George says that "the loss of a parent or husband must be deplored with blood. A finger is cut off, or the arm pierced with a sharp flint, and the deeper the incision the more sincere the sorrow." I thought it would be a way to symbolize his grief over Abigail's death.

Provincial Archives of Alberta in Edmonton. There are audio tapes on Elizabeth Boyd McDougall, Annie McDougall and Elizabeth Chantler

McDougall. There is also a copy of a speech Elizabeth gave in 1932 called "Pioneering in Alberta in 1873" from which I drew much valuable information. Her description of making and cooking bannock led to my poem "Cooking lessons," her description of her view from the hilltop the day after her arrival in Morley became "Mirage," and my found poem "Eliza's views on Indians" is taken from this speech.

I also drew on information from the following publications:

Alberta Historical Review. Calgary: Historical Society of Alberta.
Alberta History. Calgary: Historical Society of Alberta.
Historic Sites & Archives Journal. Alberta and Northwest Conference (United Church of Canada) Historical Society.

Photograph Credits

The following photographs have been reproduced courtesy of the Glenbow Archives:

Page	**Description**	**Acc. #**
Cover, p.9	Elizabeth Boyd McDougall	NA-1677-6
Frontpiece	Elizabeth Boyd McDougall	NA-2456-1
1	Elizabeth Boyd, 1872	NA-1030-25
25	Carriole and horse	NA-1406-159
27	Elizabeth and John McDougall	NA-1030-3
33	Morley Mission	NA-626-1
59	Buffalo hunt	NA-1406-7
60	Elizabeth Boyd McDougall	NA-642-14
65	The Blackfoot Treaty (Treaty 7)	NA-40-1
76	McDougall Family	NA-1030-2

The following image was used with the permission of the Clothing and Textiles Collection, Department of Human Ecology, University of Alberta:

Cover	Crazy Quilt, c. 1893	1996.25.1

(Donation of Corinne Marshall)

The following image was used with the permission of the Provincial Archives of Alberta:

32	Cross-writing	71.365/3

If you enjoyed reading *Reading Between the Lines* and would like to purchase additional copies for friends, family or colleagues, send us a cheque or money order along with the order form below.

❑ Yes I would like ____copies of *Reading Between the Lines*
@$13.95 Cdn/$13.95 US

Total $ ________

Shipping and Handling
(1-3 copies, $3.00; 4-6 copies $5.00; 7 or more,
please phone for details and discounts) $ ________

GST 7% $ ________
TOTAL ENCLOSED $ ________

Please make cheques payable to:
Rowan Books

Name: ______________________________
Organization: ______________________________
Address: ______________________________
Prov/State: ______________________________
Postal/Zip Code: ______________________________
Phone: ______________________________

Send orders with cheque or money order enclosed to:
Rowan Books
#410, 10113 - 104 St.
Edmonton, AB
T5J 1A1

Phone: (780) 421-1544 Fax: (780) 421-1588 email: jonrach@msn.com

For bulk orders and fundraising options, please contact Rowan Books.